Copyright

2020 © Bill C. Newman

All rights reserved.

ISBN:

IMPARTING BEFORE DEPARTING

ACKNOWLEDGMENTS

All glory and adoration be unto the almighty God for us unending faithfulness hitherto. Only His grace could have brought me thus far amidst all odds.

The Gospel faith Mission International (GOFAMINT) is my cave of Adullam and am eternally grateful for being a bonafide member. Words will not be enough to appreciate my spiritual father; Pastor. Taylor Karl (*Setman of Treasure youth Gathering*), Dr. Dolly (*Psychiatric Consultant*), Pastor Matthew for sharing inspiring thoughts borne out of their dealings and consistent walk with God in this book. All TYG ministers all duly acknowledged.

Unreserved celebration to Daddy and Mummy Newman & my siblings for both raising me in the way of the lord and creating a homely atmosphere to be the best I can be. A big thank you to sister Oyindamola for her relentless motivation and follow up to ensure this vision sees the light of the day. I owe you all more than I can ever repay.

TABLE OF CONTENTS

FOREWORD

In Ezekiel 37 the prophet of God was transported by the agency of the spirit into a strange location littered with dry bones. The scripture was clear about the facts that were many untold numbers of dry bones lying helplessly in that valley. The bone is scientifically the framework for the human body meaning in that valley massive decomposition of dead beings has taken place. It is worthy of note that the eventual end result suggest that whoever those people were; they obviously never earned a befitting burial after death, they never strike a chord in their lifetime and they must have died being small or never shared portion with the great(even though they had greatness tendencies) before they breathe their last.

No one could have imagined that this bone had inherent potentials and capacity which never manifested in their lifetime save for the prophetic intervention. A mighty vast army came out of dry bones thanks to the anointed prophet. In the same vein, I present this book as a prophetic message to everyone currently in the valley, ordained great but living small to come up hither. Great men congregate on mountains and died a honorable death after they have served their generation. No one owes a valley dweller an audience but mountaineers are voice in their generation. Without mincing words there is more to you than you can imagine, you are sent to fulfill a glorious destiny.

You may be born in the valley but you cannot afford to die in the valley. Your generation is waiting for your impact

WHAT IS IMPACTING BEFORE DEPARTING (IBD)?

IBD is an annual publication inspired at impacting winning spirit, stimulating the mindset of men towards greatness and provoking God's given abilities and potentials in humanity to find expression before death closes their eye. It is launched on June 2 of every year which apparently is the birthday of the visioneer. Don't settle for less you carry in you an extra-ordinary gene of eternal excellency. Learn what it takes to live an enviable life in time in this realm of existence and also intentionally etch your name in the sand of time even when you are long gone. Happy reading

"And said unto him, Art thou he that should come,

or do we look for another?"

Matthew 11:3

CHAPTER ONE

THE JOURNEY TO IMPACT

Impact making is never impossible as the scripture is flooded with patriarchs who are testaments of that reality. The contemporary world has recorded untold number of men and women whose name has been etched on the sand of time on account of their incredible impact in life. However, we may struggle to reproduce this results and may never be historically remembered if we do not master the nitty gritty as it requires more than wishes. Impact is never sudden phenomenon nor does not happen overnight, regardless of the desperation and how long we rehearse the aspiration to lay hold of it; it may take forever to happen if we do not pay attention to its proven and time tested principles. Interestingly, impact can be reproduced effortlessly by consciously learning the process and the journey of its proof producers.

"Look unto Abraham your father, and Sarah that bare you: for I called him alone, and blessed him, and increased him." (Isa. 51:2)

Impact is neither a product of chance or luck nor does it come out of the blue spontaneously. Like every other good things it takes deliberate and conscious effort to enforce. We want to draw reference from one out of the many impact makers in the scripture so that the wisdom can sponsor a stronger resolve and also regulate our excesses in our journey to becoming the next proof producer. The character to be considered in this thought is Joseph.

JOSEPH; A PROOF PRODUCER OF IMPACT

The life of Joseph from inception to the end poses a great lesson for every potential impact maker. He lived an unusual life characterized with impeccable character, absolute integrity and godliness. To him impact is never sudden; it takes deliberate and calculated effort even from the early days of his life. His journey to impact is summarily demystified in these 5Ps.

PARENT

Joseph was raised by a lone parent as the mother died after giving birth to his only brother (Benjamin), regardless there was no flaw in his life. Without doubt it appears that he had more than physical parenting as he lived a totally different life not consistent to his background. Joseph knew the God of His fathers and had cordial relationship with Him and also was receiving instruction from Jacob meaning he had dual parenting. Little wonder, growing in a polygamous setting didn't move him nor was he wrongly influenced growing in the company of his godless half brothers.

"And the lad was with the sons of Bilhah, and with the sons of Zilpah, his father's wives; and Joseph brought unto his father their evil report" Gen. 37:2b

Almost all Jacob's son had their notorious profile and individual wicked record yet Joseph stayed undefiled. It must have taken more than physical training for him to escape corruption. Joseph resented evil and could not bring himself to silence at the sight of one because he is hell bend on making impact. Unfortunately, we are in that age and time where the end time syndrome is heavily catching up with many teens and youth. Sadly, many of them do not know God and they have despised every iota of physical training coming from their parents making them losers in two ends. Joseph had an unbroken intimacy with YAHWEH and equally holds his father's tutelage in high esteem and this is what kept him immaculate under Jacob's roof.

Lessons

- Raised by a single parent is not an excuse for failure
- It is possible to be in the company of the bad and not become one.

PIT

Joseph was thrown into the pit having been stripped of his cloth of many colour. Judah led the transaction process as he gave him away in a slave trade for 20 shekel of silver. Being sold by his half brothers is enough a lifetime traumatic experience but his stability and resiliency thereafter is a pointer that his resolution is stronger than anything. Impact makers pays attention to building internal capacity than external they need no motivation as they are always self motivated.

Lessons

- Prepare for pit in the journey of destiny oftentimes prepared by friends. You cannot afford to die there.
- Invest more on the internal than external

POTIPHAR

Potiphar's house always paint a picture that looks like the destination because it is accompanied with a level of power, influence and a degree of impact and many have been trapped therein all their life. Joseph served Potiphar's wholeheartedly and managed his house with uncompromised integrity.

"There is none greater in this house than I; neither hath he kept back anything from me but thee, because thou art his wife: how then can I do this great wickedness, and sin against God?" (Gen. 39:9)

Consider what he called word "wickedness" an average young man in our age would have seen that as an opportunity. In case you have not forgotten, even in his time Rueben defiled his father's couch to do it, Judah gave out his scepter to taste it, Shechem did not hold back against Dinah etc. it can only mean that his perspective and judgment about life is regulated from the spiritual standpoint. Leaving the scene naked without hesitation indicate how intentional he was about his preserving his colourful destiny

Lesson

- Don't be fooled by the mini influence in potiphar's house and be trapped therein, the scope of impact is transgenerational; that you cannot achieve under his roof.
- Prepare to render selfless and relentless service without holding back in the journey although it may not be duely rewarded
- Sexual immorality is a threat to impact. Avoid it at all cost
- Colouful destiny will get you untold coat of many colour place value on it by preserving it with your life

PRISON

Not all prisoners are hardened criminal while some landed there on account of just reward for their wickedness or cruelty others are merely victims of circumstances. Joseph's story goes with the latter, in a twinkle of an eye a house manger suddenly became a prisoner. In all of this he was never downcasted, demoralized or attempted suicide (that's a mindset noteworthy for potential impact maker). In no time, he became a force to reckon with and was made the overseer of the prisoners. He deployed his gifting of dream interpretation to pharaoh stewards who were fellow inmates and also poured out himself like a drink in service to others in the cell.

Lessons

- No matter the challenge face it you will surely pull through suicide is never an option
- Demand will be placed on your gift and talent in the course of the journey take time to sharpen them.
- Service does not reduce anyone the route to historical impact is through the servant-quarter.

PALACE

Everyone desires a royal atmosphere and a portion with the nobles. This is because it is accompanied with luxury unlimited and completely different from the world of a c commoner. This was nothing but a consolation for Joseph earlier horrible experience in life his gifting earned him a royal invitation and as a result earns the second powerful seat in the whole of Egypt (prime minister). His influence and impact spread across borders and neigbouring nations survives at his mercy.

"And when all the land of Egypt was farmished, the people cried to Pharaoh for bread: and Pharaoh said unto all the Egyptians, Go unto Joseph; what he saith to you, do." Gen. 41:55

Position and influence reveals people's tendencies, lustful appetite and true nature. All of this was not enough to change Joseph identity nor mar his impact mission. There was no record that he revisited every wrong done against him; ne never paid his brothers in their coin nor did he summon Potiphar's wife for open confession. Joseph lived a life void of flaws from the early days of his life, endured terrible times in the journey, wielded kingly power and influence and exercised unlimited impact in the process. He slept with his fathers after he has served his generation; nevertheless his name has been chronicled in the book of impact makers and equally forever etched in the sand of time.

Lesson

- To Judah, Joseph was worth only 20 pieces of silver but to Pharaoh he was worth a royal decoration. Worry less, you are not the problem the real problem is your valuer.

- Impact can be short-lived if not managed well. Take caution

CHAPTER TWO

UNDERSTANDING THE COVENANT

Scriptural reference: Gen 17:10-14, 1Sam 17:26

Covenant is a binding agreement between two or more personalities and it is usually sealed by blood.

In the Old Testament, God commanded circumcision in Gen 17: 10-14 and God used it as a token of his covenant between him and Abraham. As many that desireto be Israelites would have to be circumcised to come into a covenant with the God of Israel. The Abrahamic covenant was sealed with the blood of circumcision. Circumcision is usually very painful, requires shedding of blood and leaves a mark on the body of the circumcised. Gen 17: 14: He that is not circumcised shall be cut off as he has broken God's covenant. Gen 17:7 reveals that the Abrahamic covenant is an everlasting covenant and it separates the wheat from the chaff. It separates God's children from other children.

The covenant by circumcision is a **covenant of multiplication , international blessings, exceeding fruitfulness,**

continuous royalty from generation-to-generation , divine protection, possessing our possession and lastly, it is an everlasting covenant. However, it is possible for someone to carry this covenant and not know its implication or even make use of it. That was what happened to the Israelites in 1st Sam 17. Goliath, the uncircumcised harassed them day and night until the one who recognized the covenant he had with God came into the scene. David's understanding of the covenant of circumcision made him to win against Goliath. The circumcised ones are Israelites, separated unto God. It is a covenant that separates God's children in the world. The covenant is so strong that it involves your seed and even your flocks and all that belongs to you.

When a man doesn't understand the covenant, he might become a prey. When hedoesn't understand the covenant, he might become chicken-hearted and unable to make impact in his generation. When a man understands the covenant, he becomes bold and can say ''Give me this mountain''. God had to tell Joshua not to fear several times and that he should be bold and courageous as he had to make a great impact for his generation. David, the teenager, understood the covenant and he couldn't be killed by the bear and the lion, so much that he saw Goliath conquered before going to him. He said "Who is this uncircumcised Philistine that he should defy the armies of the living God" (who is greater than all the gods of Goliath put together). Other soldiers including his elder brothers saw themselves as the armies of Saul. They lost consciousness of their covenant with God and ran from Goliath. Caleb had this consciousness and he said Give me this mountain even in old age. When we are conscious and engrossed by this covenant, we will be bold enough to follow God all the way and make impacts.

We also, have a greater covenant in the blood of Jesus. The covenant in the blood of Jesus links us with the Abrahamic covenant, with or without physical/foreskin circumcision. When we give our lives to Jesus Christ, we become part of this covenant. 1Cor 11:25, Jesus said, this cup is the new covenant in my blood; so the blood of Jesus not only links us to the Abrahamic covenant, it also links us back to God. Sin makes a man lose consciousness of the covenant (1Cor 11:30) like the armies of Israel in 1Sam 17. Sin makes a man a slave to the devil, thereby affecting his impact.

1Cor. 6:17-18 tells us that sin separates us from God and when we are separated from God, we can't impact our generation the way we should. Our hearts should be circumcised also (Acts 7:51, Rom 2:29). We should have the mind of Christ. The scripture says, *let this mind be in you which was also in Christ Jesus*. Joseph understood the covenant, refused to toil with sin and he was able to impact his generation. He understood that the covenant meant he should remain holy to be on the side of God. Despite the promises of God to Joshua, Ai (a small town) defeated Israel because of sin of harboring the accursed thing.

Col 2:31. Our covenant of circumcision is no longer made with hands. When we put off the body of sin, we become the circumcision of Christ and we have a working covenant with Christ Jesus, we can take the world for Jesus. Ps 2:8 "*Ask of me, and I shall give thee the heathen for an inheritance, and the uttermost parts of the earth for thy possession.*"Let us understand that the covenant we have in Jesus makes us triumph (Col 2:15). With the consciousness of this covenant in Christ Jesus, we can take the world for Jesus, we can dare the bear and the lion, we can do what ordinary people cannot do, we can dare what they can't dare, we can impact our generation.

If you want to have an impact before departing, you need God beside you. Follow his precepts, have the understanding of the covenant and triumph in Christ Jesus, triumph in the work he has called you to do without fear. We do not have the spirit of bondage again to fear, but we have received the spirit of adoption whereby we cry Abba Father. There are many obstacles on the path of impact, but with the covenant in Christ Jesus, we can overcome them. Let us be conscious of the covenant. Every word he tells you should be noted. When he says "go", please go, because he will be with you. Do not doubt his words. Please note that his words and promises to you are covenant words and just as those words came to pass for Abraham, it will also manifest in your life if you remain in God and don't break his covenants. (*Abide in me, and I in you as the branch cannot bear fruit of itself except it abides the vine; no more can ye except ye abide in me.)*

Finally, the covenant is meant for Children of God. The Christians who have been washed in the blood of the lamb. Do you want to join this wonderful clique? Why don't you repent and ask the Lord Jesus to forgive you all your sins and waywardness? Sincerely tell him to wash you with the precious blood of Jesus. Accept him as your personal Lord and Savior and by doing this you automatically become a covenant child of God. If you said this prayer, kindly start attending visit a bible believing church and introduce yourself as a new believer. God bless you.

CHAPTER THREE

THE MYSTERY OF DUALITY

Text: Matthew 16:16 – 22

"15–16: he saith unto them; Butwhom say ye that I am? And Simon Pater answered and said, Thou art the Christ, the son of God,

22-23: then Peter took him, and began to rebuke him, saying, be it far from thee Lord: this shall not be unto thee. But He turned and said un to Peter, Get thee behind me, Satan: thou art an offence unto me: for thou savourest not the things that be of God, but those that be of them."

Many a times as believer we ask some questions that are serious about our lifes and others as well. It was a great surprise to for me to detect that after our salvation we can still act in flesh if we are not careful. A lot of things are going on in the body of Christ that are funny. You see a born again believer in some mess as it were and he or she can't explain the reason for that. You can actually love God and serving Him and yet you are manifesting some strange life

The answer is not farfetched it’s the **Duality of Nature**

In the above text. Peter who just confessed Jesus went ahead on the spot and was used by Satan. Its actually funny when we see ourself doing some things and we are at times tired. You can preach against fornication for example with passion and see yourself fall into the same weeks after. This does not cancel the fact that you are not saved or you don't love God it is still you manifesting two natures in the same life.

I have seen preachers of high repute, believer on fire as it were with secret bondage on the duality of life.

WHAT IS DUALITY?

1. It is being in the Spirit and switching to flesh.
2. It is been hot and been cold at a time.
3. It is the side of our life that is not yet crucified

Samson was carrying about a great fire yet he was sleeping around with ladies. How come of him. Its simply a dual life. Peter was a great Apostle yet he was possessed, David was a messenger of grace and holiness but he later fell for what he hated.

What is happening here as I was saying its two beings living in one man.

WAYFORWARD

At any point in time we must understand that sanctification is not once and for all

We must keep evacuating our life of our sinful old man via the blood and grace that the cross made available for us. Your impact in life and destiny will be threatened if caution is not taken in this regard. The values you built for years can crumble overnight if you perpetually allow the flesh to interfere or overtake you. The following are ways to stay consistent and arrest duality in your life forever

i. Always live by the spirit (Gal 5:16)

ii. Be a prayer and fast addict (Luke 18:1)

iii. Be word-full

iv. Avoid godless company (1 Cor. 6:33)

v. Mind transformation (Rom 12:2)

You are obviously on your way to becoming the joy of many generations if you can do these. May your name forever become an household name. see you at the top.

CHAPTER FOUR

THE FORBIDDEN LAND

(A no go area for every impact maker)

In your quest for knowledge, impact and relevance in life there is a land you must neither pitch your tent nor share habitation therein. In a bid to make end meet in destiny you must not consider spending the night talk less of taking residence in a strange land called the forbidden land. This land has wreck untold havoc many of which are undoubtly irreversible to her inhabitants. Countless number of great dream, world changing ideas and global vision has been successfully swallowed by the land.

Innocent pilgrims who were on a mission to make historical impact who not only plight her route but made a brief stopover in this land has paid more than what they bargained for . Many lost their lives in the land and the few who were lucky enough came out disarmed of every impact potentials and as a result could not amount to anything in life.

"The greatest loss is not death, the greatest loss is what dies in us when we live." Anonymous

Lot and his two daughters made the greatest mistake of their lives by retreating to a small city called Zoar as against the instruction of escaping to the mountain. Even though they left the city but it was obvious things were not the same again in their lives (they left Zoa but Zoa never leaves them). The virgin daughters have been initiated into another knowledge contrary to God injunction as they slept with their father on the ideology that he was the only surviving man on the planet. Interestingly, God only wiped out Sodom and Gomorrah not the entire world as it were. This can only be a clear indication that they have partook of the forbidden fruit in the forbidden land.

The forbidden land is tempting and inviting on the outward look but characterized with untold misfortune on the inside. The sadder reality is that it has never suffered crowd as people walk in there every now and then either on a temporal or permanent stay. However, it is indeed noteworthy that it is a land to be wary of and unsafe for habitation for any potential impact maker that even passing a night there can corrupt one's enviable destiny owing to the many threats domiciled in the land.

THREATS IN THE FORBIDDEN LAND

1. The Size of the Land

"Behold now, this city is near to flee unto, and it is a little one: oh, let me escape thither, (is it not a little one?) and my soul shall live." Gen. 19:20

One peculiar characteristics of the land is the smallness of its border and bandwidth. Hence, the first stronghold of the land is the size. The configuration of the forbidden land is smallness and as a result it is alien to greatness and will fight anything that look like one. Lot had greatness tendencies by virtue of identifying with the Abrahamic convenant and he was definitely going somewhere to happen as he was already gaining divine attention until he entered the forbidding land. Although, it appeared he came out alive but it was obvious many things had became lifeless in him. The land is without mincing word capable of reducing a giant to an ant

2. Forbidden Fruit

Every region or places on the planet earth is identified with their unique food. The forbidden land is no exception as it feeds every of her inhabitants with an unusual food called the forbidden fruit. The forbidden fruit has the capacity to initiate you into another knowledge that is not consistent with the knowledge of God.

"And he said, who told thee that thou wast naked? Hast thou eaten of the tree, whereof I commanded thee that thou shouldest not eat? " Gen. 3:8

Even God had to ask Adam the source of his latest information in his knowledge bank as that must have been gotten elsewhere. In the wisdom of the triune God nakedness is alien to God's design for man and only a corrupted wisdom could have brought that knowledge. The judgement of Lot's undefiled daughters equally became corrupted owning to the strange knowledge and committed incest as a result.

3. Inhabitants of the Land

Quality relationship must be embraced in the journey of destiny as it significance to timeliness of fulfiment and impact. However, wrong relationship can be devastating and inimical to destiny especially if one of party is from that accursed land.

One quick way to identify a dweller of the forbidden land is their thought pattern, nature and character. The following are some of their dominant trait which include;

i. They resent greatness and will talk it out of anyone who have one

ii. They are both small and negative in their thinking

iii. They despise or think less of others

iv. They are confident in their foolishness

v. They are perfect examples of failure

Conclusion

The forbidden land is synonymous to many things like: wrong marital relationship, ungodly association, wrong church, wrong business group, wrong environment etc. and has oftentimes left indelible scars on persons who are victims of these experiences if they are ever alive to tell the story. without argument it is a no go area for anyone who cherishes his/her destiny, God given vision as they can be strangled or truncated by overnight and the rest is an history. If you have seen any of these above mentioned indices around your life or circle of influence take the next available flight,come out by wisdom and escape to a safer zone (Zion). See you at the top

www.ingramcontent.com/pod-product-compliance
Lightning Source LLC
LaVergne TN
LVHW020541160826
845677LV00015B/4152

* 9 7 9 8 8 4 2 6 6 4 1 8 4 *